Boot Hill Stories

Boot Hill Stories

Silver Fever on the Frontier

By
RaNae Morris Travers
and
Karen Wilkes

Publisher: Karen E. Wilkes
Nevada@dmartnevada.com
Cover and design by Darryl Martin

ISBN 978-0-578-56794-5

Acknowledgement

When writing either fiction or non-fiction, it is a sure thing that you are not doing it alone. Nothing occurs or is created in a vacuum.

In our case, writing about Boot Hill would have taken us several years, if we had not been following in the footsteps of the meticulous researcher, Leo Schafer.

This book could not have been written without the liberal usage of Leo Schafer's books – *"Boot Hill, The Pioche Cemetery" and "Law and Disorder in Pioche."* Historical research is a very tedious game of inches, and it takes very serious discipline.

Friedrich Nietzsche once said, *"Of all that is written, I love only what a person hath written with his blood."*

Therefore, we take our hats off to Leo Schafer and beg his forgiveness for the over-usage of his books, as he truly exemplifies the above quotation. In many cases his research was all that we could find on our subjects. Fortunately, we have been able to add a few facts that were previously unknown.

We sincerely hope that our efforts with these stories will further the understanding of those adventuresome folks who made their way to the Western frontier – with the stop in Pioche turning into their last.

Dedication

Bryce Travers, Austin Travers
And
Levi Benton
(Those who came after us)

And

(Those who came before us)

Datie Elizabeth Peterson, great grandmother of RaNae Travers, raised seven children in the mining camp of Frisco, Utah—a town so wild and lawless, a wagon picked up the dead bodies in the streets every morning and transported them to the cemetery for burial.

Maud "Betty" Wilkes, grandmother of Karen Wilkes, followed her miner husband for 12 years from mine to mine over four western states. She was widowed in 1930 in Pioche with children, ages 10 and 12, where she remained until her death. Pioche was her last stop.

Introduction

RaNae and I met at the beginning of the third grade in Pioche, Nevada. It was at the tail end of the last mining boom in that community Post World War II. Our parents, of course, had no idea that this last boom would quickly turn into "borasca"—an old mining term for "bust"—and that the town would soon wither.

The entire country was booming and our fathers, both of whom had seen action during the war, were feeling mighty lucky to have returned home uninjured. With the optimism of all young returning servicemen, they started new careers, bought houses, and settled in with their wives and young children. Coincidentally, RaNae's house was about two blocks west of Boot Hill cemetery and mine was two blocks south!

As young girls, we played dolls, draped ourselves creatively in our mother's 1950's circular skirts, and wandered the high desert adjacent to our houses— somewhat mindful of our parents' warnings, "You kids be careful to watch for glory holes and rattle snakes!"

Those played-out glory holes left by ambitious and adventuresome miners of the past, along with weathered, metal mine carts, rusting tramways, dried timber mine shafts, great piles of sedimentary tailings, and, of course, Boot Hill cemetery became our neighborhood parks. We spent our weekends and summers looking for purple bottles, examining old tin tobacco cans, and wondering, "Was it true that there was big money coming in from the East, and the mines were going to open again?"

Pioche was a very remote mining boomtown. The boomtowns of the California gold rush along the Sierras and those along the Colorado Rockies were closer together, and there was more movement between the towns, facilitating communication from the outside world. Whereas, Pioche was 343 miles from Salt Lake City and 428 miles from Reno, creating a Petri dish for extreme behavior – extreme independence, extreme innovation, extreme survival instincts, and extreme violence. As the town matured with the development of the mining industry, the rough edges of its citizenry were honed along with the millions of tons of raw, silver ore coming from the depths of the mines. Gradually, family life became the norm, as the Henry rifle and hand guns were gradually replaced by hunting rifles, and as most of the gunfighters were laid to rest in the Boot Hill cemetery to live on through legends only.

Pioche remains hundreds of miles in every direction from any freeway. Although inconvenient at times for adults, children are as free as they ever were to roam the high desert, digging for hidden treasure, tromping through Boot Hill cemetery reading gravestones; and, oh yes, carefully watching for glory holes and rattle snakes.

RaNae and I feel privileged in every way to have numbered among those children, and to have inherited from this colorful background a strong sense of independence, freedom of thought, the ability to find humor always (let's face it, our Pioche ancestors were a pretty entertaining lot), and the confidence to know that if you can survive in Pioche, you should be able to survive anywhere.

Hopefully, the joy we have experienced in sharing this project and the heart we have for our hometown will shine through the telling of these **"very true"** stories of those men and women— some innocent; some not; some of good character; some not; some very clever; and some not—who found their way to the legendary boomtown of Pioche.

Contents

The Cemetery

By RaNae Morris Travers

This book tells the stories of some people who died in Pioche in the late 1800's and were buried in Boot Hill cemetery. Or were they buried in the Pioche public cemetery? Research indicates there is no difference. In Pioche, the terms "Boot Hill" and "cemetery" both refer to the Pioche public cemetery. The cemetery must have been established in March 1868 when saloonkeeper Frank Pitt was fatally shot by Jacob Colburn. Mr. Pitt was the first person buried in the public cemetery. By 1873, the public cemetery had more than a hundred graves. Women and children were buried there, but most of the graves were for adult males. Many graves were for victims of mining accidents; but during that period of time, 30 men died as victims of homicide. The public cemetery did have a loosely defined segregated area called "Murderer's Row". Although exact burial places were not recorded in the 1800's, it can be assumed that Murderer's Row was reserved for gunslingers, claim jumpers, and, of course, murderers. Because many of the men buried in the cemetery died with their boots on, sometime in the past the cemetery was given the "Boot Hill" nickname.

The *Pioche Daily Record* described the cemetery in 1873. There were "*Rude headstones with inscriptions written in pencil.*" Many graves had "*nothing to indicate the name or nativity of the dead.*" Approximately 25 graves had actual headstones. One hand carved wood grave marker recorded, "*Shot by a coward while working his claim no one even knew his name. Pioche Nev.*" The *Record* also complained, "*The public cemetery ought to be enclosed, for it is no credit to our camp that its dead should be interred in an open field.*"

It is not true that 72 people died in gunfights and were buried in the cemetery before anyone died of natural causes. The reality is interesting and more diverse. The first 72 burials include 4 people who were believed to be poisoned by unclean water, one pneumonia victim, a possible cholera victim, and eleven men who died in the horrific fire of September 1871.

The Pioche public cemetery, also known as "Boot Hill", is movingly evocative of the mining camps of the American frontier. The cemetery is directly underneath an aerial tramway, original to the mining operations of the 1920's and 1930's. The buckets sway in the wind on thick cables. Almost a hundred years ago, those buckets carried silver and nickel ore from the mines to the Godbe Mill. If you visit the cemetery, you might hear, above the silence, the sound of mine bells, the noisy machinery of the mills, and laughter coming from saloons.

Antonio Cardinos (Miner)

By RaNae Morris Travers

Died: October 5, 1873
Pioche, Nevada
Cause of death: Shot by Charles Peasley

On June 26, 1870, Antonio Cardinos was living in
Hamilton, White Pine County, Nevada working as a miner.
He was 38 years old. The 1870 United States Federal Census
records his birthplace as "Mexico". A question in the census
for the first time lists his parents as "...of Foreign Birth".
Four months later, he was in Pioche where he was indicted,
but not convicted, for the killing of R. H. "Kit" Carson. This
would not be Mr. Cardinos' first link to the Pioche cemetery.
Three years later, he would be buried there.

In November 1870, the *Clear Lake Courier,* Lake County,
California reported:
*"A man known as Kit Carson, nephew of old Kit Carson, was
found dead in the street of Pioche City, beyond Hamilton, Nevada, on
Sunday, with several bullet holes in his head and body. It is supposed
that he was murdered."*

It is not known whether R. H. Carson of Pioche; or Tom
Carson, sheriff of Abilene, Kansas; or other young men on
the frontier named Carson who claimed to be nephews of Kit
Carson actually were. However, the "old" mountaineer and
famous Indian fighter was the 6th of 10 children, so it is
possible.

The body of R. H. "Kit" Carson was holding a pistol in
hand. The first report was uncertain—suicide or murder?
The decision was murder, and several people were arrested.
One of them, Mr. Kernew, blamed Antonio Cardinos for the
murder. Because Mr. Kernew's statement was not allowed as
evidence, Mr. Cardinos was not convicted. Mr. Kernew
jumped bail and fled to Mexico.

On October 5, 1873, Antonio Cardinos was dead in the Union Saloon on lower Main Street in the Chinatown area of Pioche. He was lying on the floor of the saloon with a white handkerchief over his face. A friend sat near, fanning the flies away. Cardinos had been shot by Hartwell Charles Peasley. Hours before, in the early morning, four men had been in the saloon. The bartender, Joseph Leflower, was serving drinks to Antonio Cardinos, Charles Peasley, and Jim Moran. Cardinos and Peasley had had some small troubles in the past.

An argument between the two began when Cardinos called Peasley a coward and dared him to go outside and fight. The argument did not appear to be about anything. It escalated, however, fueled by the late hour and alcohol. "*Coward*" turned into "*cur*" and "*s-o-b*". Peasley asked Cardinos, "*Why are you down on me?*" Cardinos answered, "*I'd like to fight you! And you're no man!*" The bartender interrupted them saying, " Pioche *There's no use of you old-timers here in Pioche wrangling about this little thing.*" Finally, Cardinos stepped back from the bar with a drink in his left hand, his right hand behind him under his coat. Cardinos may have wanted Peasley to think he was armed; but there was no evidence Cardinos had a pistol or a knife.

It was reported in the *Pioche Daily Record* that sometime before this bar fight, Peasley confided to a friend that Cardinos had threatened to kill him. Peasley was afraid of Cardinos. When Cardinos stepped away from the bar, Peasley pulled out his pistol and fired twice at Cardinos. Cardinos staggered back into a chair and died in a few minutes. His right carotid artery had been cut by one of the bullets. He was Burial #198 in the Pioche cemetery.

The shooting was considered self-defense, and Charles Peasley was acquitted.

S. D. Potter (Saloon owner).

By RaNae Morris Travers

Died: May 8, 1873
Pioche, Nevada
Cause of death: Shot by Jefferson Howard

Surely, S. D. Potter is the only person buried in the Pioche cemetery to have been killed by a bullet passing through a stove. S. D. was the proprietor of Potter's Saloon on Meadow Valley Street, not the best saloon in Pioche.

S. D Potter died in his saloon on the evening of May 8, 1873. The *Pioche Daily Record* reported,

> "*Last night, about eleven o'clock, S. D. Potter...was shot and instantly killed by a negro named Howard. Howard and two other colored men were playing cards in the saloon. Some say Potter himself being engaged in the game with them.*"

An argument began and Potter ordered Jefferson Howard to leave. Howard refused. Potter is reported to have said, "*You damn son of a bitch, if you don't leave here I'll put a hole through you.*" Howard was unarmed. Potter told him to go heel (arm) himself.

The *Pioche Daily Record* continued, "*A few moments afterward Howard appeared at the door, hailing Potter with 'Look out there now. I'm going to turn loose.'* " The shooting began. Howard was standing at the door. Potter was at the back of the saloon, behind a large box-stove. They were about 20 feet apart. The fifth or sixth bullet fired by Howard passed through the stove, striking Potter in the heart. Potter was killed instantly, and Howard took flight. He was chased by the customers in the saloon. Although a lynching was threatened, Howard was arrested in a house on Cedar Street by two deputy sheriffs and taken to jail.

Alcohol, late hours, and combustible tempers caused many of the burials in Pioche's Boot Hill cemetery. S. D. Potter was burial #165.

In 1870, three years before Jefferson Howard shot S. D. Potter, four adult African American men lived in Lincoln County. Only one of them, a porter named H. Johnson, lived in Pioche. Jefferson Howard was not one of the four. Western American mining camps were ethnically diverse; but the economic class structure was rigid. White men owned and ran all of the mines. Poor white men, Mexicans, and Chinese were the miners, working in the shafts. A few African American men, who left the southern states after the Civil War, worked in the mines; but most worked in service jobs. Jefferson Howard, who had been a Union soldier, came to Pioche after the summer of 1870, likely dreaming of earning his fortune in a rich mining town or at least getting steady work. Instead, he was found guilty of manslaughter and received ten years hard labor in the state penitentiary. He was pardoned after about half of his sentence. In 1880 he was arrested in Lyon County (Nevada) when, during an argument about a horse race, he pulled his gun on a state assemblyman.

Joseph Thomas (Miner)

By Karen Wilkes

Died: January 2, 1874
Cause of Death: Homicide

Joseph Thomas was born in Cornwall, England in about 1837. (During the 1800's in the British Isles, births were not always reliably recorded, and many records were lost. Some birth dates were approximated based on baptism records retained by the churches.)

Cornwall had been a major producer of copper and tin for several hundred years, but when the price of copper fell in the mid 1800's, the industry tanked. Between the years of 1861 to 1901, 250,000 residents of Cornwall, mostly miners, left the U.K. to find work elsewhere. Many of these miners found their way to the western United States where they were hired immediately for their skills and experience gained in the Cornish copper/tin mines.

One of these skilled miners, Joseph Thomas, had travelled to the remote mining camp of Pioche, Nevada, undoubtedly due to rumors of its mega sized discovery of silver on Treasure Hill. He was hired by William Rosemurgey (sp) on a contract basis at a mine in the Highland District.

Working on a contract basis, versus working for wages, generally provided a financial advantage for an experienced, industrious miner who could produce more ore per hour than the average. Joseph Thomas was undoubtedly one of these higher producing miners; however, this advantage quickly turned into a disadvantage due to a dispute with his boss over his wage.

The population of these mining camps in their infancy – 1861 to 1880—was made up primarily of immigrants and Civil War veterans. There was a severe shortage of women. The miners were mostly young single men working twelve-hour shifts in the mines with little time and few healthy outlets for letting off steam after these intense, long shifts underground. They had no families, no T.V. and no internet. The bars filled that void, and there were plenty of them.

Alcohol flowed through these towns like raging rivers; and due to the Civil War, there were plenty of guns and men who knew how to use them – lots of alcohol, everyone was packin', and the air was filled with testosterone. Pecking orders automatically developed during the working hours in the tunnels and carried over into the dinking hours in the bars, creating overly-heightened senses of honor among the men. What could go wrong?

During the evening of the first Sunday in November, Thomas Symons was tending bar in his saloon, "Wells and Symon's Saloon," located on Meadow Valley Street. Joseph Thomas happened to drop by that evening, as did his employer, William Rosemurgey (sp).

Rosemurgey approached the bar and requested a drink, but was turned down by Symons, the bartender, who told him he had had enough. Thomas then ordered a drink and asked Rosemurgey to join him—they drank together for a spell. So far so good! However, at some point in the recent past, there had been a delay in payment of wages to Thomas, which had remained a sticking point between these two men.

Romurgey: *"If you want to attach that money, you can attach it and be damned."*

Symons, the bartender, weighing in: *"We're not talking about attaching the money, the thing was not mentioned."*

Rosemurgey: *"If you want a game you can get one from me."*

Thomas: *"I ain't afraid of your game."*

Rosemurgey started backing out of the saloon, drawing his pistol as soon as he stepped outside. A bystander then touched his wrist and told him to put his gun away. Rosemurgey complied and put the gun back in a pocket. (Holsters were very rare and not used much at that time. Guns were concealed in clothing – coat pockets, pants pockets, or waist bands.)

Thomas: *"Let him pull that damned thing out."*

Rosemurgey rose to that unfortunate challenge and re-drew his gun. Thomas quickly turned and ran, but it was too late. Rosemurgey, fully fueled with alcohol and carrying a loaded gun, shot Thomas in the back when he was no more than five to ten feet away.

Fortuitously, officers, Knerr and Fat Mac MacKee, were on the opposite side of Meadow Valley Street, and were able to quickly apprehend Rosemurgey and arrest him. Thomas was sent to the Pioche hospital.

Joseph Thomas, shot in the back over a very insignificant wage dispute, fueled by alcohol, gun powder, and unfortunate ego challenges, lingered for two months in the Pioche hospital. He rallied several times, but finally succumbed to his wound. He passed away on January 2, 1874 and was laid to rest in the Boot Hill cemetery—Number 214.

William Rosemurgey received a sentence of fifteen years in the Carson City state prison. He was pardoned after eight years, as were most murderers during the mid-1800's. It was very difficult for the prosecution to keep their witnesses in line – most witnesses were not above spinning their testimony in favor of the accused—often because they were being paid off, and sometimes just because it was the Wild West and they wanted it to stay that way! Also, many members of the juries had the exact frame of mind—their heightened sense of honor when in a bar fight, quite often did not transfer to court cases—taking a bribe, or telling a white lie under oath, just didn't seem that bad out on the frontier.

At about this time, the *Pioche Review* printed a quote from one of the local Indians, "*White man hep kill 'em too much in Pioche.*"

Charles Hickey (Lawman)

By Karen Wilkes

Died: October 2, 1872
Cause of Death: Gunshot

October 8, 1872, the *Pioche Review* reports, *"SHOOTING IN THE STREETS* - Mr. *Holland, the Fire Marshal, and who has been volunteering as a night watchman, informs us that there was a number of shots fired on Meadow Valley street this morning about one o'clock, and that it was almost a miracle that several people were not killed or wounded. He felt the need of assistance, but there was none at hand."*

Now, in 1872 in Pioche, there was no shortage of male ego among the outlaws, nor was there any shortage among the lawmen either. Apparently, Charles (Charley) Hickey, an officer of the law, wandered into Lynch's Saloon the evening of the 7th; whereupon, a buddy, John Crowley says, *"Did you see that item in the Review?"*

Hickey takes the paper and starts perusing the article when, who should enter the saloon, but the author of said article, Mike Holland, the Fire Marshall. Hickey says to Mike, *"Did you put this in this paper?"*

Holland says, *"No."*

Hickey, *"You must have given the item, as it reflects on me."*

Holding up the bar that fine October evening was Sheriff John Pattie who later added, *"They talked somewhat rough to each other, when I interceded, and told them it did not amount to much and to let it drop."*

Mike Holland, feeling a bit bruised and compromised, issued an ultimatum, *"Come outside and I will fight you."*

Sheriff Pattie:

"He started for the door, drawing his pistol as he did so, and as he drew the pistol....it discharged. I rushed out after Holland,.....'Mike, for Christ's sake let it drop'. As I grabbed Holland, Hickey came out of the upper door with his pistol in his hand."

Hickey, *"You damned cur."*

Holland, *"You are a damned big loafer."*

28

Pattie, "*They both then commenced shooting…I saw Hickey afterwards; he had a wound in the breast about the heart, and he had one in his side.*"

Hickey's funeral party with eight pall bearers and close to 200 mourners processed from the courthouse to Boot Hill. A subsequent inquest determined that Hickey's death was, in fact, caused by the bullets from Mike Holland's gun, but there was no indictment. In fact, within six months, Mike Holland was promoted from Fire Marshall to Fire Warden, and in four more months he was appointed as deputy by Sheriff, Wes Travis.

In brief, Pioche lost a much-needed officer of the law when Charles Hickey was gunned down by the Fire Marshall. However, as luck would have it, the Fire Marshall, Holland, lived to replace his victim, so that the Pioche Police force was once again fully staffed. Apparently, no one in Pioche found those circumstances to be out of line or odd! And, if they did, they decided the best policy was to keep quiet about it. After all, there were a lot a stray bullets flying around Pioche.

The Women

Pioche, Nevada and the Western Frontier

By RaNae Morris Travers

Pioche, Nevada and the Western Frontier

In 1870 Pioche was still a very young mining camp, a mining camp in its infancy. And, like the wider early American frontier surrounding them, the early mining camps essentially attracted two types of women: married women following their husbands and young women planning to make their living as prostitutes.

The 1870 census recorded 1,134 people living in Pioche. Only 54, approximately 5%, were women eighteen or older. Fifty of the women answered that their occupation was "keeping house". Eight of those fifty were suspiciously young, unmarried, and living alone. Four were "Hurdy Dancers" living at a saloon. Regardless of occupation, none of them could have had an easy life in the mining camp. The *Pioche Daily Record* described the town during spring runoff, *"... the mud is becoming a serious impediment to travel by vehicle, on horseback, or on foot. There is a reeking mass of rubbish, decaying refuse, and offensive decaying matters."* There was no river, stream or water system of any kind. All of the women would be trying to stay clean, wash clothing, mop floors, and cook. Some would be tending babies and trying to teach small children to read.

In time, conditions on the western frontier mellowed, changed, and adapted. Women, anxious for the economic choices that were almost uniquely western, left the east. Some hardy and self-sufficient ones became station agents for the railroad or stage coach, telegraphers, boarding house owners, newswomen, and ranchers or farmers. Others were teachers, midwives, and nurses. Nevertheless, even on the frontier, the ideal woman was still considered a homemaker. The reality was different. Long after the passing of the western frontier, a 1943 survey concluded that western women were still affected by the frontier experience. They were often well educated, held untraditional jobs, worked longer before retiring, and approved equal standards for men and women.

What a difference ten years makes. Pioche also reflected the changes occurring on the frontier. The 1880 census recorded 751 people living in Pioche, a reflection of the downturn in mining activity. 136 were women eighteen or older, approximately 18% of the population. Eleven women had occupations other than "keeping house". There were seamstresses, washer women, servants, a teacher, a dressmaker, a milliner, and a lodging housekeeper. Page 6 of the census gives us proof of the real change in the economic opportunities for women on the frontier and even women in mining towns. The entry on Page 6, line #43 was for Eliza Lawson, a 45 year-old widow, whose occupation was "*keeps butcher shop*". Eliza Lawson was a survivor and a success.

Fanny Peterson (Spanish Courtesan)

A "Spanish courtesan", prostitute, or "upstairs girl"

By RaNae Morris Travers

Died: July 12, 1872
Pioche, Nevada
Cause of death: Shot by Lyman P. Fuller

The life and death of Fanny Peterson is a classic story of prostitutes in the American West. In lawless, isolated mining towns, homesick miners pined for women. Many single women of the time had no economic options. They came west and entered prostitution as a business decision, a decision with harsh results. Few made enough money to retire; and their lives were often ended by suicide, drug overdose, illness, or murder. Venereal disease was common.

Fanny Peterson referred to herself as "a Spanish courtesan", maybe to earn more for her services. Brothels on the frontier charged more for Caucasian up-stairs girls than for Chinese, black, or American Indian girls. "Spanish" does not appear on any of the brothel menus in the four brothel museums of the American West; but it may have seemed exotic and economically beneficial to Fanny. There is, however, another explanation. The Library of Congress has a late 1800's Mexican newspaper containing an advertisement for a cigar and tobacco factory. The three Mexican girls sketched in the advertisement are called "Spanish Beauties". Fanny Peterson may have been Mexican or even Panamanian.

Fanny Peterson was murdered by a man who had been her lover, Lyman Perry Fuller. According to the *Daily Alto California* newspaper, Fanny and Lyman were known to have violent quarrels. They were not living together. A year before her death, Lyman tried to burn her possessions and made several attempts on her life. On the morning of July 12, 1872, Lyman saw Fanny on the street as he was leaving home. He fired three shots at her. His first bullet shattered her right arm. Fanny collapsed in the street. Lyman fired the next two bullets as he stood over her. The second bullet missed her. The third went through her hip into her stomach. Lyman seems to have momentarily considered suicide as he put his pistol in his mouth. Then he pointed it toward the ground and fired.

Fanny Peterson died later that day after accusing Lyman of setting the Pearl Saloon on fire five weeks earlier and poisoning the hogs of a local farmer. She was the 80th burial in the Pioche Cemetery.

Lyman P. Fuller was arrested and sentenced to fifteen years in the penitentiary at Carson City. He was pardoned after eleven years, light punishment for the ruthless murder of Panama Jack.

Minnie Summers (Actor)

By RaNae Morris Travers

Died: October 28, 1873
Pioche, Nevada
Cause of Death: Suicide

Minnie Summers, whose stage name was Mary E. Chapman, was a twenty-five-year old actress from Philadelphia. In 1871, after a brief stay in California, she moved to Pioche. On October 26, 1873, she attempted suicide by drinking an ounce of laudanum. At the time, laudanum was called "tincture of opium" as it contained 10% powdered opium. It was a working-class drug, largely taken by women. Men abused alcohol. Although the alcohol content was about 48%, laudanum was cheaper than a bottle of gin or whiskey because it was considered a medication and not taxed as alcohol. It had been commonly used since the 16th century to treat pain and coughs. It was not used by physicians to stop breathing; but that is what an overdose of laudanum does.

It is not known whether Minnie Summers was a laudanum addict when she came to Pioche or whether she bought her first bottle of laudanum in Pioche because she knew it was an effective way to commit suicide. In 1873, laudanum was sold without a prescription; it would not require a prescription until 1914. Miss Summers could have purchased her bottle of laudanum in Pioche or any town or city, from any doctor or pharmacy, simply by asking for it.

Initially, Miss Summers was lucky. She was treated at the Pioche hospital and regained consciousness. She said she wanted to live. Recovery seemed possible; but thirty-eight hours after she drank the laudanum, Minnie Summers died on October 28, 1873.

The report of her death in the *Pioche Daily Record* makes it clear that Minnie Summers had been working as a prostitute during her time in Pioche. The newspaper called her death,

"...*the self-wrought death of a poor girl whose ways had ceased to be the ways of virtue and pleasantness and the rash importunity of whose desperation and remorsefulness had brought her to a sudden impulse to take a leap into death's mystery.*"

Her graveside services, conducted by Rev. Henry L. Badger, were "*attended by a large number of women of her own class in carriages.*" Minnie Summers was the 205th burial in the cemetery.

Fred Wagner (Mill worker)

By Karen Wilkes

Died: November 1872
Cause of Death: Mill Accident

We know that men from all parts of the world and walks of life were represented in the mining camps of the West, stretching from the Rocky Mountains of Colorado to the gold country of California; north to Bozeman, Montana and south to Tombstone, Arizona. The lives of a few of these men were documented in mining records or newspapers, but many came to the camps, worked hard, drank harder and left unnoticed.

Fred Wagner's death was published in the *Pioche Review*, but other than that, we know nothing about Fred Wagner. I am of the mind that he was an industrious and forward-thinking man. He had found his way to a very remote mining camp in order to take a job in a mill which paid quite well for those days – almost as much as underground miners who were making $4.00 per day.

Fred had also brought his wife and two children with him. Many mine workers would travel to these remote areas to work, but would leave their families in more established, safer towns offering schools and hospitals. Fred had made a conscious decision to keep his family with him in Pioche regardless of the lack of civilized amenities.

The mining in Pioche was all underground. The ore was extracted by blasting areas of rock, supporting the cavity with timbers, and hoisting the rocky debris to the top in buckets.

At that point, the rocks had to be shipped in wagons to the new mill in Bullionville, about ten miles south of Pioche, where the rocks would be crushed into sand size particles. The sand would then go through a smelting process with the application of chemicals and high heat to separate the precious metals from the gangue (worthless sedimentary by product.)

Fred Wagner worked at the Magnet Mill on the midnight shift - which generally meant a twelve-hour shift.

The *Pioche Review* reported,

"*Two men were at work in the mill when the last candle burned out. One of the men went upstairs for fresh candles leaving the other, Fred Wagner, alone in the dark with the machinery. One of the belts had broken and Wagner was in the process of repairing it when his clothing was caught, and he was pulled into the machinery and crushed to death. A thorough search was made, but his head was never found.*"

Fred Wagner's remains were the 107th to be laid to rest in Pioche's Boot Hill graveyard. It is assumed that his widow and two children returned to their place of origin to be with family.

The Weapons

By Karen Wilkes

The Chinese started experimenting during the 9th century with a combination of saltpeter, charcoal and Sulphur, resulting in black powder, which they tamped into bamboo shoots and metal tubes—creating the first guns. This invention was immediately used for protection and was traded along the silk road, making its way to Europe and to the Americas. Each war from then on provided the impetus and the money to fund further refinements to all firearms and cannons.

By the mid 1860's, the time of the western gold and silver rush, pistols and rifles had become readily available due to a marked increase in manufacturing during the Civil War. Between 1848 and 1873, the Colt Company turned out 21,000 revolvers, knows as "Revolving horse pistols." Many of which found their way to the California gold camps.

A further advancement was made by the manufacturer of the 1860 Colt Army revolver, of which 200,500 were produced for the Civil War. Thousands of these guns made their way west, as soldiers were allowed to purchase them directly from the Army. Also, Smith & Wesson introduced a popular single-action six shooter in 1870.

The introduction of the vest pocket Deringer was a real game changer. In fact, this was the gun used by John Wilkes Booth to assassinate President Lincoln. It could more easily be concealed in clothing than any other gun on the market. Contrary to Hollywood movies, almost all revolvers were carried in pockets or waist bands, as the holster was not invented until the 1920's.

During the Civil War, soldiers took great pride in owning a Henry Rifle, often called "sixteen shooters,"— the chamber held that many rounds. Many infantry soldiers purchased a Henry with their re-enlistment bonus, as they figured the Henry's high rate of fire could save their lives. Confederate Colonel, John Mosby called it, "*That damned Yankee rifle that can be loaded on Sunday and fired all week.*" Historians argue that one man armed with a Henry was equivalent to 14 or 15 men equipped with single-shot guns. It's not hard to figure how valuable a Henry would be to any man living in Nevada during the mid-1800's.

The most versatile and economical firearm for hunting and defense was the twin-barreled scatter gun, used by ranchers, stage coach guards "riding shotgun," and lawmen. The best balanced and favorite six-shooter of its time was the Colt single action army revolver released in 1873, which became an instant favorite with lawmen, settlers, and bandits. As we've mentioned before, there was a fine line between these three classes on the frontier.

In 1873, the *Pioche Record* noted, "*A man sneezed in the presence of another yesterday, and the other did not even draw his Whistler...*" Edward Whistler had just released his new English patent pistol which had become the rage in Pioche – a very fast six-shooter, which could release all six rounds in rapid succession.

In short, many male residents of Pioche owned one of the above guns, but certainly not more than one. Guns were expensive, ranging from $2.50 to $3.00 and upwards to $10.00 for a special model. Therefore, when a man arrived in Pioche with a" Henry" rifle <u>and</u> a six-shooter, all eyes looked his direction, as it was a sure sign that another "gunfighter" had arrived.

Pierpont Thayer (Actor)

By RaNae Morris Travers

Died: September 18, 1873
Pioche, Nevada

The grand opening of Brown's Theatre in Pioche, which later
became Thompson's Opera House, was held on September
16, 1873. Bella Bird's Players, an acting company from San
Francisco leased the theatre for the opening. Miss Sallie
Hinckley and Mr. Pierpont Thayer were the principal
attractions. Their performance in the comedy *"Pygmalion and
Galatea"* was a great success. Pierpont Thayer had a good
career, appearing in California and Nevada. In 1867, he was a
30-year-old actor living in San Francisco at Broadway and
Montgomery streets. In February 1873, he played at the
Carson Theatre and Piper's Opera House in Virginia City.
Mr. Thayer and Miss Hinckley arrived in Pioche on
September 10 on the Hamilton stage coach. It had been
expected that on the evening of September 17, the day after
the grand opening, Mr. Thayer would be a featured player in
"The Fortunes of a Poor Young Man"; but his part was played by
a substitute actor.

Late in the evening of September 18, 1873 moans were
heard coming from Mr. Thayer's room at Mrs. Caldwell's
lodging house on Meadow Valley Street. His door was
locked and access was finally gained through his window.
The men who entered the room found Pierpont Thayer lying
on the floor undressed except for an undershirt. White
frothy foam covered his mouth. An empty bottle of
laudanum (opium) was on a table. Mr. Thayer had been
drinking for two days and was in the habit of taking
laudanum when he drank. The laudanum bottle held just one
ounce; but laudanum and alcohol were often a deadly
combination. Some reports state he had lost his position
with the acting company. He left a note written on sheet
music. The words were, *"I test the problem. Pierpont Thayer"*.
Two days after the grand opening of Brown's Theatre,

Pierpont Thayer was dead and would be the 196th burial in the Pioche cemetery.

In 1908, Gelett Burgess (1866 - 1951) wrote *The Heart Line,* a book about the spiritualists, fortune tellers, and outright con artists who worked in San Francisco before the 1906 earthquake fundamentally changed the city. In Chapter VII of *The Heart Line,* there is a discussion about Pierpont Thayer:

> " *'I was just a-thinkin' about Pierpont Thayer. Don't*
> *you remember that dope who went*
> *nuts on spiritualism and committed suicide?'*
> *'No, I don't recall it, what about it?'*
> *'He got all wound up in the circles here---Sadie Crum,*
> *she had him on the string for a year,*
> *till he didn't know where he was at. He took it so   hard*
> *that one day he up and shot hisself*
> *and left a note pinned on to the bed that said: I go to   test the*
> *problem. I would have sold every one of   my tricks and all of hers to*
> *him for a five-dollar bill!   Why didn't he come to me to test his*
> *problem?'*
> *'......Them that want to believe are going to, and you   can't*
> *prevent 'em no matter what you do.*
> *They're like hop fiends----they've got to have their   dope*
> *whether or no, and just so long as they*
> *can dream it out they're happy.' "*

Pierpont Thayer did not shoot himself. But Gelett Burgess added an intriguing third possible cause for Thayer's suicide: alcohol, laudanum, and, perhaps, spiritualism.

Joseph Lynch (Chop house owner i.e. Steakhouse)

By Karen Wilkes

Died: July, 1873
Cause of Death: Homicide
Gravestone: -"Shot During a Dispute Over a Dog"

FRANK SCHOONMAKER:

"I was in Lynch's Chophouse at about one or two o'clock in the morning of the sixth of July." (He was accompanied by his pet dog.)

"About the time we had finished our lunch, I noticed that Sullivan, whom I did not know at the time, had my dog by the back, and raised at arm's length above the table; he then let it drop; I immediately got up, and going to their table, asked him what he meant by abusing the little dog." He remarked that he didn't know whose dog it was, and did not mean to hurt it. Mr. O'Neil then arose, remarking that it did not matter whether the dog was hurt or not. Then Mr. Lynch remarked to O'Neil that he had better not have anything to say about it. I then said to Sullivan that as long as he did not intend hurting the dog, we would let the matter drop and have nothing more to say about it, which seemed to be mutual; I walked out of doors, followed by the other four."

"....meanwhile Sullivan and I were talking the matter over in a friendly manner, when O'Neil came back to the door, and, pointing his finger at Sullivan called him a damned coward; then Sullivan said something about the dog, whereupon I hit Sullivan in the face; we clinched and he jammed me against the closed door. Just as we clinched I heard a shot. The first thing I recollect after that was seeing Lynch lying on the sidewalk....I then felt blood trickling down my side, which was the first intimation I had that I was shot."

"Before we clinched I stood within two or three feet of Sullivan, Harrington was to my left about three or four feet up the street from me....I saw a movement of Harrington's elbow – simply throwing his elbow up. Immediately after I saw the elbow movement, I heard a shot which came from my left. I heard only one shot."

WILLIAM WEBER (The Chophouse waiter):

"I heard a shot, went to the door and heard a second shot, which I saw Harrington fire into the crowd. I then turned to go back again, and as I turned I saw Lynch fall: I then heard a third shot...."

JAMES SPURLING:

"I was in Charley Strum's Saloon; heard an altercation outside and went to the front door and, looking towards Lynch's Chophouse, I saw Schoonmaker, and a man pointed out to me as O'Neil, wrestling. I saw two men standing on the sidewalk, and Lynch sitting on a stepladder along side of the saloon. I saw Schoonmaker's cane fly up as O'Neil was backing him in to the restaurant. Lynch jumped off the stepladder, drew a pistol out of his pocket and commenced to beat O'Neil over the head.

"One of the other men rushed in – to separate them. I suppose. Immediately after that I saw Harrington fire a shot into the crowd. Either Sullivan or Harrington, I don't know which, got Lynch from O'Neil. They all seemed to separate...then...Harrington fired another shot...Lynch said: 'Don't shoot any more: I'm killed.'"

EDMUND O'NEIL:

".....I went out first, Schoonmaker next, asking me what in hell I had to say about his dog. I said nothing more than I had been telling my partner that he had made him act the coward. He said 'that's none of your business you son of a bitch.' And raised his cane and struck me on the head making a wound there. –I- heard Harrington say 'Lynch what in the hell do you strike that man for?' Lynch was to my right; I turned around knocked against the building and saw a pistol in Lynch's right hand. He said to Harrington 'God damn you, if you move I'll shoot the head off you.' Schoonmaker and I were now scuffing the shooting then commenced. I heard Sullivan say 'Hold on Lynch, don't shoot.' I heard five or six reports of pistols – no less than five. I don't know who fired the first shot."

57

OFFICER WOODRUFF:

"....I arrested him (Harrington) and took his pistol from him; found three loads discharged."

Within several minutes, Harrington shot his pistol three times resulting in five wounds – one through Sullivan's wrist, one in Schoonmaker's side, one in O'Neil's side, with Lynch receiving a wound to his shoulder and a fatal wound to his head. Did the bullet which went going through Sullivan's wrist project into Lynch's side? Did the bullet that hit Schoonmaker; project through him and into O'Neil, or could there have been a second shooter? Modern forensics could have solved these questions.

Aside from all of the conflicting testimony about how this totally senseless shooting happened, the bottom line was that during the early morning hours of July 6, 1873, in Pioche, Nevada, three men were wounded and one man killed over the questionable treatment of a small dog. John H. Lynch, a married man in his early thirties, had resided in Pioche for two or three years, leaving his widow, a resident of San Francisco. Due to the hot July weather, John Lynch's body was not shipped to the widow in the Bay area.

The shooter, James Harrington, is an enigma. He really had no business even being in this gun fight. It wasn't his dog. The argument was primarily between Lynch and Sullivan with O'Neil inserting himself in a supporting role. None the less, James Harrington fired three rounds from a loaded weapon hitting four people.

Harrington was known for his hot temper, and rumor had it that he had killed three men. He was found guilty of murder in the second degree. Prior to being sentenced he attempted to break out of the Pioche stone jail. The walls were about two-and-one-half feet thick, but dismantling a thick stone wall was no problem for a Pioche miner, who was the recipient of several smuggled tools—a pinch bar, a file and a case knife.

After the failed jail-break attempt, Harrington was sentenced to fifteen years in the Nevada State Penitentiary. He lost several appeals, but was pardoned in about a year. This seems a likely ending for this story; but, unfortunately, it does not end here. James Harrington and John Sullivan, probably traveling together as friends, appeared again in Virginia City less than two years later.

However, the supposed friendship came to a screeching halt when the two got into an argument—Sullivan was falling down drunk—and Harrington shot him in cold blood four times. He received a twenty-year sentence, but was pardoned again!

Some years later in Idaho, Harrington kicked a dog - of all things - and was killed by R.A. Cunningham, the dog's owner. Now that is truly a most literal take on the subject of "karma!"

John Lynch was the 180th resident of Pioche to be laid to rest in the Boot Hill cemetery.

Frenchy Danis (Pioche resident)

By RaNae Morris Travers

Died: November 5, 1873
Pioche, Nevada
Cause of death: Stabbed by Robert McCullough

Some of the bodies buried in the Pioche Boot Hill Cemetery arrived there with knife wounds.

All the components needed for a fight to turn deadly were at Schultzbacker's Dance House on Meadow Valley Street on the evening of November 5, 1873. There was a drunk man who slapped an innocent by-stander and then was stabbed by a man with a knife. Edward "Frenchy" Danis entered the dance house shortly after midnight. He had been drinking and near the entrance, he slapped the face of a man named Mucahy. Mucahy had a defender, Robert McCullough, who said, "*This is a quiet and inoffensive man.*" McCullough pulled a pocketknife and said that Frenchy was drunk. Words were exchanged; Frenchy told McCullough he could have a fight. Frenchy left the dance house after slapping his hand on the bar and saying he cared for no one.

Frenchy returned to Schultzbacker's where McCullough was standing by the bar holding his open pocketknife. McCullough suggested, "*Come, let's have another dance.*" Frenchy said, "*Well I don't give a God damn for you.*" McCullough answered, "*Well I don't suppose you do Frenchy.*" Frenchy's final words were, "*McCullough, I've got but one hand [his left was bandaged] but it's a God damn good one.*"

Frenchy punched first. McCullough punched back holding his open knife. He hit Frenchy in the throat and blood streamed out. McCullough turned and handed his knife to William Soule. McCullough ran out the front door of the dance house, back in the front door, and out the back door. He was pursued by Ben Hyde and James Davis. Hyde caught him in a drug store. He was arrested by Officer Kelly.

Kelly asked McCullough why he had cut Frenchy. McCullough answered, *"I didn't cut him."* Then Kelly asked, *"What did you run for?"* *"I didn't run."* was the reply. *"I guess"* said Kelly *"you're mistaken, for I ran after you."* McCullough was arrested and taken to jail.

Frenchy died. McCullough was released on bail. He returned to work. In early 1874, still out on bail for knifing Frenchy, Robert McCullough's eyes were seriously damaged by an explosion in the Raymond and Ely's main shaft. He left Pioche seeking medical help and never returned.

From March 1868 through December 1875, more than forty people were shot with guns and buried in the Pioche Cemetery. In the same period, only five men were stabbed and buried. One was the 26-year-old Canadian, Edward "Frenchy" Danis, the 207th burial in the Pioche cemetery. Stabbings were less common than shootings, but the results could be just as deadly.

William McKee (Sheriff)

By Karen Wilkes

Born: May 27, 1834 (South Carolina)
Died: February 23, 1882
Cause of Death: Bronchitis

William L. Mc Kee was born on a farm somewhere in South Carolina to John Mc Kee, a farmer. I could not determine the identity of his mother, and feel that she probably died very young, as the 1850 census shows William, age 16, living with his father, a presumed step-mother, and a number of siblings at W.C River, Bibb, Alabama.

I could only find one William L. Mc Kee who joined the Confederate Army in South Carolina. I'm quite sure after checking out a number of Mc Kee's that this is one and the same. He served as a private in the Infantry Regiment— Holcombe Legion, Company F. This Legion helped to defend Charleston, S. C. in the summer of 1862, but I was unable to successfully trace his service any further. The Confederate records are not as complete as the Union records.

William L. Mc Kee is absent from the 1870 census, but it is certain that he arrived Pioche in the early 1870's. The first mining claim was filed in Pioche in 1864, but it took a few years before investors arrived to finance the development of the mines. The initial big silver boom ran primarily for five years (1870-1875.) The growth of the town was so dramatic, the lifestyle of the prospectors and early miners was so rough, and the town was so remote, that a lawless climate existed into the 1870's.

The first sheriff, Rogers, was appointed in 1866 and lasted four months. James E. Mathews served 15 months, followed by C. W. List and William Ritter. John Kane was elected November 1870 and lasted to 1872; Wes Travis served 1872-1874; and Andrew Fife 1874-1876. William "Fat Mac" McKee had served as a deputy sheriff under Travis and Fife before he was elected Sheriff in 1876. McKee really took to this job and was definitely the right man at the right time and place. He served three consecutive terms.

He may have gravitated toward law enforcement due to his military experiences during the Civil War. He might have discovered, as many men did, that he had talent with fire arms, and he must have been a very large man, quickly gaining the moniker of "Fat Mac." One thing is sure, Fat Mac had what it took to keep the Pioche roughs in line.

An example of McKee's style was reported in the *Pioche Review*, Feburary 1873:

"In Justice Court – Joseph Noble got on the rampage, night before last and declared war against everybody in general and nobody in particular – he was war like on general principles, as the boys generally are when they imbibe too freely...."

"Officer Fat Mac McKee confronted Mr. Noble and successfully arranged a suspension of hostilities. Noble spent the night in jail and was fined one dollar and costs the next day."

This was a run-of-the-mill evening for Fat Mac; however, he had his work cut out for him when some of the toughest gunslingers in the West rolled into town. Around 1870, there was a trio of tough guys causing trouble around Pioche—Morgan Courtney, Barney Flood and Michael Casey. On some occasions they were professional gunslingers hired to protect mining claims—which made them legitimate "gunnies" according to the prevailing laws of the time. On other occasions they were just tough gunslingers without portfolio.

Courtney, an Irish immigrant, most probably served on the Union side during the Civil War, where he would have honed his firearm skills, developing speed and accuracy.

In August of 1873, Morgan Courtney and George W. Mc Kinney had a shootout over an "upstairs woman, i.e. a working girl" named Georgie Squires. Courtney, who had won numerous gun battles during the preceding years, was shot in the back by McKinney and died that evening from the numerous wounds.

Neither Courtney nor McKinney were known for their good character in the community, but both men had a following from the local bars. Sheriff Travis had allowed the accused, Mc Kinney, a full measure of freedom around the jail and the courthouse. Several of Courtney's followers were demanding that the sheriff tighten up security and treat McKinney like the "accused murderer" that he was. It was also rumored that this group was leaning towards organizing a lynching of McKinney.

One member of this group, J.C. Ross testified at McKinney's trial that McKinney had told him he planned to take a shot at Courtney, and that he, Ross, had warned Officer McKee of this.

In response to this accusation, Deputy Fat Mac McKee testified at the trial, *"Not that I recollect."*

Later, another Courtney fan, John Manning, remarked to others that Deputy Mc Kee was one of Sheriff Travis' pets, and that he had assisted in the killing of Morgan Courtney. The next morning, McKee disarmed several members of this group; however, Manning was still drinking and wandering the streets when their paths crossed.

Manning: *"Hold on, Mac, I think you're a friend of the party that killed Courtney."*

Fat Mac: *"What have you got to say about it?"*

"Nothing, Mac, but I don't like officer's that murder a man."

"You are drunk now. Any difference we have had we will settle when you are sober. Go to bed, and when you get sober, I'll talk to you."

"Mac there's no damned son of a bitch in this town can make me go to bed. I'll go to bed when I'm ready."

After a few more exchanges between the two men, Manning appeared to be going after his pistol. McKee was sober and faster. He fired, and Manning fell to the sidewalk.

Manning was transported to the local drug store where a doctor examined him. His boots were removed right away, because it was considered at that time to be an insult to die with your boots on. Manning died about a half-hour later. Officer, Fat Mac McKee, was arrested for the shooting of Manning and $10,000 bail was set. Sheriff Travis and others posted his bail. The grand jury saw no reason to indict McKee, and the matter was dropped. McKee was elected Pioche Township Constable about a year later and County Sheriff after that.

Most of the characters in this drama were of Irish descent, and several, if not more of them, had served in the Civil War—with at least one serving on the Union side and one or more serving with the Confederacy. I can't help but wonder if war loyalties played into any bias on either side of these gun battles.

On a lighter note—the *Pioche Daily Record, October 31, 1873:*

"Wednesday night at 11:00'clock officer McKee arrived from Bullionville, bringing with him Geo. Chandler accused of stealing a pair of pantaloons. Yesterday Chandler went before Justice Van Hagen and demanded a jury trial..."

Chandler was sentenced to seventy-five days in the county jail for stealing the leather pants. This does seem reasonable since they were leather!

On December 27, 1875, Officer McKee took a wife, Malissa Radford of Millard, Utah Territory. According to the 1870 census, Malissa was born in 1861 to John W. and Leah Radford, which would make Malissa 14 years of age at the time of this marriage. (Pioche is about 50 miles from the current boarder with Utah.)

By 1880, five years later, the census shows William L. McKee married to Lizzie McKee, also born in the Utah Territory in 1861. I could not locate a record of this marriage.

What happened to Malissa—had they divorced? McKee was age 46 at the time of the second marriage and Lizzie was 19.

According to Ancestry.com, Malissa, the first wife, married Joseph Huff in 1885 in White Pine, Nevada. Joseph was also born in Millard, Utah in 1865, so he and Malissa would have been child-hood friends. They remained married until Malissa's death in 1922.

Sheriff, William "Fat Mac" McKee, continued to successfully fight the toughs, roughs and gunnies of Pioche until he became ill with bronchitis and passed away February 23, 1882. He had served his community well and had undoubtedly prevented many more incidents of violence than did occur, saving numerous lives. He was 47 years old at the time of his death and was buried in Boot Hill Cemetery.

Morgan Courtney (Gun fighter)

By Karen Wilkes

Died: August 1, 1873
Pioche, Nevada
Cause of death: Homicide

By 1870, mining production in Pioche was full-out; drawing young, eager men of all types anxious to make their fortunes. One of these was Morgan Courtney, described by an associate,

> *"...a gentile-appearing man; quiet and reserved. He came to Pioche from Salt Lake. On his arrival he handed three hotel checks to the hotel clerk and asked him to have his baggage sent from Salt Lake. When the baggage came it proved to be a small satchel, a Henry rifle, and a six-shooter, each article bearing the name of Morgan Courtney."*

Not all miners rode into town armed, so a man ordering the delivery of two guns from Salt Lake was automatically introducing himself as a gunslinger, or as sometimes called a "rough." In these mining camps a gunslinger could be for hire by a mining company to protect their claims—basically legal protection. Or, it could mean he was for hire by claim jumpers, or that he was a claim jumper—illegal protection.

Many of these "roughs" were immigrants—a large percentage Irish, and some were orphans, left to fend for themselves on the streets of New York or Boston. Also, the Union Army had rigorously recruited young male immigrants as soldiers directly from the Irish famine ships, where they became proficient in the use of firearms, learned basic battle techniques, and were faced with the violent deaths of other soldiers. Morgan Courtney could well have been one of these Union Army recruits.

Within months after arriving in Pioche, Morgan Courtney had hooked up with three buddies, or they had known each other from some prior community—Michael Casey, Barney Flood and William Bethers. The four entered

72

into a contract with the Raymond and Ely mining company to remove the Newland brothers, claim jumpers, from the Washington and Creole mine, owned by Raymond and Ely. Courtney and company tricked the claim jumpers by ordering a case of whiskey to be delivered to the mine as if by accident. The guards took the bait and proceeded to tie one on, ending up dead drunk by 3:00 A.M. Courtney and boys then jumped the wall with guns blazing, and after a significant gun battle regained the Washington and Creole mine for the rightful owners. Courtney received a slight wound in the battle, but healed quickly. On the claim jumper side, ten were wounded and two were thrown down a 70 ft. mine shaft.

After that battle, Courtney became a man of some significance in town—now being known as "The Chief,"—common vernacular for "fastest gun in town." He was also by this time carrying himself as a "dandy" of sorts. He had developed fine tastes in clothing and jewelry. He ordered black suits of the finest broadcloth, white linen shirts, and sported pick-pointed boots and manicured fingernails—quite something to be noticed in a wild and wooly, remote mining camp.

He was purposefully transforming his persona from an Irish immigrant to that of a very successful mine owner—sort of. Perhaps Courtney was one of the first to understand you have to dress for the job you hope to achieve, and his philosophy was working, as he was garnering a substantial following among the fast moving "bar" crowd in Pioche.

Morgan Courtney was born in Caharciveen, Kerry County, Ireland, probably sometime in 1842. Ireland did not issue birth certificates during the 1800's, so the only documents available to establish a person's birth was a record of baptism. Most Irish at that time only guessed at their age. Morgan Courtney, as he introduced himself in Pioche, was actually baptized as Richard Moriarty in December of 1842, sponsored by his parents, Michael Moriarty and Johanna Courtney Moriarty. The Irish in the 1800's did not use middle names or initials, which adds to the difficulty of establishing identity, but all evidence points to this Richard Moriarty being one and the same as the Morgan Courtney from Pioche.

Richard Moriarty had killed a bartender in 1868, in Virginia City, Nevada, over a drink order; had successfully out-run the law; and, according to Charles Gracy, a Pioche mining engineer, Courtney had told someone in Pioche that he had returned to Ireland for a spell before changing his name to Morgan Courtney and re-surfacing two years later in Pioche—418 miles from Virginia City. Name changes to avoid the law was not uncommon in the West at that time.

A search for Richard Moriarty in Civil War records, turns up only one soldier by that name, who joined the Union Massachusetts Infantry, mustering in for 90 days service on August 5,1864 for duty at Fort Pickering, Salem, Massachusetts, and mustering out November 12, 1864—and again, re-upping for one year at Salem and mustering out June 30, 1865. We cannot be certain that this is the same Richard Moriarty, but the likelihood is high.

It is with this probable background of Civil War service; a childhood in Ireland—a country still reeling economically from the potato famine; enduring hardships and perhaps violence in order to survive in the tough Irish neighborhoods of New York or Boston, that Richard Moriarty, now known as "Rick" found his way to the mining camps of the newly discovered western territory.

On a chilly day in November, 1868, Rick had showed up at the Niagara Dance Hall on B street in Virginia City. Between dances, he walked to the neighboring saloon and ordered a glass of wine. The bartender poured him a glass of whiskey.

"I asked for wine," Moriarty objected.

Whereupon, the bartender adopted a look of disgust, and retorted, *"Whiskey is good enough for the likes of you."*

Moriarty squared off as to punch the bartender, when a bystander, John O'Toole grabbed his arm, saying, *"Watch it, my lad, or you'll be feeling the might of Irish knuckles."*

Moriarty, pulled out his revolver, probably from a pocket, as holsters weren't used at that time. He backed out of the bar, walked around the building, and then took a shot at O'Toole through a glass window, severely wounding him. O'Toole died three days later, and Moriarty vanished. Some say he fled back to Ireland. Others say that he was in Montana. We only know that in 1870, Morgan Courtney arrived in Pioche, Nevada, on the Salt Lake to Pioche stagecoach, appearing identical to the Richard Moriarty of gun-fighter fame in Virginia City.

After the Pioche gun battle at the Raymond and Ely mine in 1870, Courtney shot his next man, James Sullivan, in 1872 over challenging words in Clancy's saloon. The two men stepped outside of the saloon, exchanged more words, and according to Courtney, Sullivan started to draw a knife, so he shot him at close range through the heart, killing him instantly. After the shooting, Sullivan's knife was found to be still fully encased in his sheath. Courtney was indicted, spent the summer in Lincoln County jail, but was acquitted by a jury—not unusual in Pioche.

Even Courtney was surprised by this one, and was afraid to be seen on the streets, but this was short-lived, as his identity had been revealed to the lawmen in Virginia city, who sent word to re-arrest him for the 1868 murder of O'Toole. He was sent back to Storey County to be indicted and tried; however, due to a lack of witnesses available to testify, Courtney was once again released from a capital offense. This Irishman's four-leaf clover was working over-time!

In 1873 in Pioche there were very few single women and a very large number of single miners, mill workers and gunslingers. Working girls of the "red light district" were in much demand, and they needed to earn a living—not good odds for a young "gunnie" to demand fidelity from a local prostitute.

It was now known openly in Pioche that Morgan Courtney was really Richard "Rick" Moriarty, but he was now a superintendent of a mine conducting business under his new alias. Courtney had been seeing local working girl, Georgiana "Georgie" Syphers (Scyphers) and had developed an attitude of some exclusiveness regarding their relationship. After all, Courtney had a good job, dressed very well, spent money lavishly, and had a firm reputation as "Chief" in the town – meaning you better think twice about challenging Courtney in any manner.

However, coincidentally, at about that time, a newcomer, George W. Mc Kinney, road into town, by way of Elko, where he had been employed as a "watchman." A watchman was usually paid to guard a mine, and it was a job demanding if any person tried to trespass, the watchman was to shoot to kill and ask questions later. It was reported that George Mc Kinney was a darn good watchman (meaning that he was a good shot and not slow to draw.) However, he was also known to be addicted to both whiskey and laudanum, an opiate.

Mc Kinney also took up the acquaintance of Georgie Schyphers, creating a triangle of combustible elements. Naturally, Courtney called Mc Kinney out and basically ordered him to leave town. Mc Kinney who was suffering from an intestinal disorder, decided that he would not leave town and would confront Courtney head on. He borrowed a gun (a Whistler six-shooter—a new and much-desired model) and went in pursuit of a showdown, trusting that he had the better gun and was the better shot.

Mc Kinney fired two shots at Courtney facing him on the street. Courtney was not able to retrieve his gun from his pocket fast enough (the hammer probably stuck in the fabric, which was a common problem) and turned to run when Mc

76

Kinney fired four more shots into his back at close range—maybe three to four feet—catching his coat on fire.

Courtney had cut a wide swath through the fast-moving town of Pioche. He was laid to rest August 1, ~~19873,~~ after a long procession of three hundred citizens led by his cousin, William Kelly, followed by Rev. Father Monteverde, a brass band, the Hook and Ladder Company and the Hose Company.

George Mc Kinney was arrested, indicted, and after a jury trial lasting ten days, the jury deliberated ten minutes and acquitted, George W. Mc Kinney—again, not unusual in Pioche.

Richard Moriarty's funeral was impressive, but he was buried in Boot Hill (#186) in an unmarked grave. The *Pioche Record* reported,

"Morgan Courtney (the name by which he was known in this community) feared by some, detested by others, and respected by a few, was a desperate character......We only refer to his tragic death as a verification of the prophesy that those who slay by the sword shall by the sword be slain."

Earl Wilson Hamilton (Saloon owner)

Cousin of Alexander Hamilton

By RaNae Morris Travers

Died: March 13, 1876
Pioche, Nevada
Cause of death: Stabbed by John Rice

On March 14, 1876, the *Pioche Daily Record* reported
*"Pioche is in mourning. One of her foremost, most useful and public
spirited citizens lies in the cold embrace of death."* Pioche mourned
for Earl Wilson Hamilton who had been fatally stabbed by
John H. Rice. When he died businesses and saloons closed.
The newspaper printed an original poem calling him Pioche's
"brightest light" and a *"friend in every way"*. The Lightner Hook
and Ladder Company resolved that his name would always
remain on the roll of the Company and that their
headquarters and apparatus would be draped in mourning for
thirty days. The Pioche Fire Department required members
to wear a badge of mourning. After the funeral at the
Episcopal Church, a band and most carriages in town
accompanied the cortege to the cemetery. The eight pall
bearers were four Odd Fellows and four firemen. At the
cemetery, the members of the I.O.O.F. performed the
Order's service for the dead.

Earl Wilson Hamilton was an unusual mining camp
resident and saloon owner. He was born in 1833 into two
distinguished American colonial families. His father was a
cousin of Alexander Hamilton, the first Secretary of the
Treasury. His mother was related to John Randolph of
Roanoke who was a member of the U.S. House of
Representatives, the U.S. Senate, and served as U.S.
Ambassador to Russia. Earl lived with his parents in
Davenport, Iowa until 1859, when he joined a prospecting
expedition headed for Colorado. For the next decade, he
mined and freighted in Colorado, Idaho, and Montana.

In 1870, Earl and his wife, Emily, were living in the small
mining camp of Silver Park, Nye County, Nevada. He listed

his occupation as engineer. In 1872, their only child, a son, was born in Pioche. On the 1875 Nevada state census, Mr. Hamilton was a Pioche resident and a "liquor dealer".

Every witness at the inquest essentially told a similar story and agreed that Earl Hamilton was stabbed in his saloon by John H. Rice who used a Bowie knife. Mr. Rice was an agent and man-of-business for Wells Fargo and for Sherwood Bros. Earl Hamilton and his half-brother, Alfred C. Hamilton, rented a room, to be used as a keno parlor, from Sherwood Bros. with Rice as the rental agent. The revenue from the keno parlor did not justify the rent. Although Mr. Rice reluctantly lowered the rent, the Hamilton brothers ended the contract. On the afternoon of March 9, 1876, Rice came to the saloon and demanded the small amount of rent owed to him. Earl Hamilton put $7.50 on the bar. Rice pushed $3.00 back, saying he owed it to Alfred Hamilton. The verbal exchange between them became heated and angry. Earl Hamilton signed a statement saying,

"Noticing that Rice was mad about something, I asked him what was the cause of his madness. He replied, 'You know well enough what it is.' I remarked I did not. He then said you are a d----d-----, anyway.' At the same time he shoved his hand down inside his vest and withdrawing a white-handled knife. Rice kept approaching and finding that he would cut me I struck at him with a spanner, hoping to keep him off when he at the same time struck at me with the knife, cutting me in the left side. Other parties present interfered and shoved Rice out into the street, when I succeeded in getting away from those who were holding me and went to the door after him, but he was taken off down the street by an officer. I then went around the counter and got a pistol and again came to the door, but was held back by other parties. I then walked across to the drug store and had my wound dressed."

Three days later, Earl Wilson Hamilton died from that wound on Sunday, March 12th.

The anger between Hamilton and Rice is not easily explained. They had been friends and may have shared lodging for a short time when Earl Hamilton moved to Pioche. On March 21, 1876, the *Carson Daily Appeal* reported,

"*Rice gave himself up to the Sheriff, but there being no money in the Lincoln treasury to procure sustenance for prisoners, he was allowed to go on his own recognizance. After the death of Hamilton, the excitement ran high, and Rice thought it prudent to leave town for a short time. Accordingly he took the stage for White Pine, arriving yesterday, when he at once reported to Sheriff Raum, informing that official that he had no idea of fleeing the country and that he would return to Pioche whenever he should be wanted for examination....Hamilton was a man greatly Rice's superior physically.*"

At Earl Hamilton's request, Rice was not prosecuted; and he returned to Pioche. On April 29, 1876, the *Eureka Daily Sentinel* mentions him passing through Eureka on a "westward bound" business trip. On October 11, 1876 the *Pioche Daily Record* reported that John Rice would be in charge of the Pioche Wells Fargo & Co. office for a week

After Earl Hamilton died, two Nevada newspapers, the *Virginia Chronicle* and the *Carson Daily Appeal,* published false stories about the stabbing. The *Pioche Daily Record* called their stories, "*Not True.*" and went on to say,

"*... (two newspapers) published horribly incorrect versions of the difficulty between J. H. Rice and the late Earl Hamilton. Scarcely a single incident as stated by the above papers is true, except the names of the parties and the unfortunate termination of the affair. The story published by the Virginia Chronicle and the Appeal is as follows: 'Last evening a dispatch was received by a gentleman of this city to the effect that John Rice had fatally stabbed Earl Hamilton in Pioche. This unfortunate occurrence is reported to have been caused by Rice attempting* *to introduce a disreputable woman into a ball-*room, *of which Earl Hamilton was floor manager. Hamilton ejected Rice and his partner, whereupon Rice pulled out his bowie knife and stabbed Hamilton to the heart. He died almost instantly....Rice is well known in Eastern Nevada. Since his arrival in this State he has been in the employment of Wells, Fargo & Co., and has been generally liked and respected. His only fault seems to have been a weakness for the opposite sex...'"*

This deceptive version of the stabbing stubbornly persists in the historical records.

Less than two weeks after Earl Wilson Hamilton was buried in the Pioche Boot Hill Cemetery, the *Pioche Daily Record* reported:

"The body of Earl Hamilton was yesterday exhumed. J. Ward, the undertaker, took charge of the affair and had the casket containing the body conveyed to his undertaking establishment on Main Street, where the casket was placed in a zinc lined box and made ready for shipment by this morning's Salt Lake stage. Eugene Blair will accompany the body as far as Beaver, Utah and will see to its further shipment. The destination will be Davenport, Iowa, the case being marked to Davenport Lodge, I.O.O.F., Davenport, Iowa."

We do not know for certain where Earl Hamilton was buried in Pioche or what his burial number would have been. But it is fair to say that after eighteen years on the western frontier, Earl Wilson Hamilton might have preferred to stay buried in Pioche. He is, instead, buried in Oakdale Cemetery, Davenport, Iowa. Not all the bodies once buried in Pioche are still there.

Boot Hill Cemeteries
Here and There

Not every western American town had a public cemetery nicknamed "Boot Hill". It required a lot of violent deaths for a cemetery to be called "Boot Hill". The first Boot Hill cemeteries were in the cattle towns of Hays and Dodge City, Kansas. Many of the cemetery occupants were cowboys who "died with their boots on" in gunfights, beatings, stabbings, and hangings. There are other famous Boot Hills in Tombstone, Arizona and Deadwood, South Dakota.

Boot Hill cemeteries began as public cemeteries. The first victim likely arrived at the cemetery with a fatal gunshot wound. But it wasn't long before gunfighters, claim jumpers, and cowboys were buried next to housewives, farmers, judges, miners, and children.

The Pioche Boot Hill cemetery is not unique. It is, instead, an absolutely classic example of a Boot Hill of the American west. It began, and continues to be, the local public cemetery. Between 1868 and 1875, 269 people were buried here. For the most part, the gunfighters are buried next to the gamblers. People who came to Pioche for the silver strike may have thought they would eventually be going down the road to the next mining discover. However, hundreds of them are buried in Pioche and could not make that choice. The silence, the smell of sagebrush, and the sounds of the historic tram add to the solemnity of the cemetery. Real people with dreams and aspirations were buried here.

Pioche Boot Hill Cemetery: Bibliography
Sources used by RaNae Morris Travers
and Karen Wilkes

Bagley, Will,   With Golden Visions Bright Before
Them; Trails to the Mining West 1849 - 1852.
2012. University of Oklahoma Press,
Norman, Oklahoma.

Burgess, Gelett. The Heart Line. 1908. Reprinted
2016 by Wentworth Press, W. Columbia, South
Carolina.

Convis, Charles L. Outlaw Tales of Nevada. 2006.
Morris Book Publishing, LLC.

James, Ronald M. and James, Susan A., A Short
History of Virginia City. 2014. University of Nevada
Press, Reno, Nevada.

Myres, Sandra L., Westering Women and the
Frontier Experience 1800 - 1915. 1982. University
of New Mexico Press, Albuquerque, New
Mexico.

Reeve, W. Paul, Making Space on the Western
Frontier. 2006. By the Board of Trustees of the
University of Illinois.

87

Reid, John B. and James, Ronald M., editors,
Uncovering Nevada's Past. 2004. University of Nevada
Press, Reno, Nevada.

Schafer, Leo, Boot Hill the Pioche Cemetery and
the Story of the Pioche Boom. 2008. Book
Connection, LLC, Pioche, Nevada.

Shafer, Leo, Law and Disorder in Pioche, Crime
and Punishment in Lincoln County During
the 1800's. 2009. Book Connection, LLC,
Pioche, Nevada.

NEWSPAPER:
Pioche Daily Record. 1872 - 1876. Pioche, Nevada.

Made in the USA
Las Vegas, NV
01 January 2021